The Wit *and* Wisdom *of* Downton Abbey

By Jessica Fellowes

 St. Martin's Griffin 🙢 New York

A Carnival Films / Masterpiece Co-Production
Downton Abbey™ and Downton™ Carnival Film
& Television Ltd
carnival © 2005 Carnival Film & Television Ltd
Masterpiece is a trademark of the WGBH Educational Foundation
MASTERPIECE

www.stmartins.com

Designed by Ben Cracknell | benstudios.co.uk
All photography © Nick Briggs

The Library of Congress Cataloging-in-Publication Data is available upon request.

ISBN 978-1-250-09360-8 (hardcover)
ISBN 978-1-250-09361-5 (e-book)

Our books may be purchased in bulk for promotional, educational, or business use. Please contact your local bookseller or the Macmillan Corporate and Premium Sales Department at (800) 221-7945, extension 5442, or by e-mail at MacmillanSpecialMarkets@macmillan.com.

First published in Great Britain by Headline Publishing Group, an Hachette UK company

First U.S. Edition: October 2015

10 9 8 7 6 5 4 3 2 1

Contents

Introduction

Anyone connected to *Downton Abbey*, whether creator, producer, actor, cameraman or make-up artist, is always asked the same thing shortly after they have revealed that they work on the show: why is *Downton* such a success?

It's a fair question. With hundreds of millions of viewers worldwide, the show has won multiple awards including BAFTAs, Emmys, Screen Actors Guild awards and Golden Globes. It even holds a Guinness World Record as the Most Critically Acclaimed Television Show – all of which makes it Britain's most successful export in television history.

Not only is the show watched and enjoyed by people the world over but it has become a kind of common cultural reference point. Where Brits and Americans will confuse one another with talk of biscuits, chips and cilantro, when it comes to *Downton Abbey* everyone understands each other perfectly. It doesn't seem to matter whether Violet's quick-witted remarks are pronounced in English or Russian, they still elicit the same laughter. Whether women wear mini-skirts, saris or the niqab, they swoon over the details of Lady Edith's beaded dresses equally. There's even 'the *Downton Abbey* effect', named to explain the sudden success of things which have nothing in fact to do with the show but have nonetheless enjoyed a benefit – republished books from the era hitting the bestseller lists, visitor numbers to English stately homes increasing year on year, the recent popularity of 1920s baby names, the surge of butlers employed in China. As social media has exploded in the last few years, the *Downton Abbey* conversation has taken place online between viewers watching the show from their sofas or bamboo mats.

In short, it is a show of enormous, extraordinary and phenomenal success, the like of which is probably not going to be seen again in our own lifetimes. But is there an answer as to why it works so well?

There's a cocktail of an answer, of course. When the show first began, the whole world was more or less in the throes of the recession, and it is a known truism that when we feel unsafe, we look to the past for comfort – nostalgia is a powerful emotion and *Downton Abbey*, set at the cusp of the modern age and featuring characters that could have been our grandparents or great-grandparents, delivers nostalgia in spades. It is beautiful to look at, features gorgeous stately homes, good-looking actors and covetable cos-tumes. There's a wide cast, which means that for almost any viewer there's a character they either recognise or relate to. There are two family set-ups – the blood-related family upstairs and the one that is artificially created by colleagues working closely together downstairs. We may not either have servants or be servants but we all experience similar rivalries, romances and friendships, whether with siblings, friends or co-workers. The master/servant relationship is at the core of many brilliant dramas, whether Shakespeare or Chekhov. It would take a doctorate to analyse properly, but it seems we are all still fascinated by the boundaries set and blurred between employer and employee.

My uncle, Julian Fellowes, creator and scriptwriter of *Downton Abbey*, believes it is such a successful show because the audience enjoys watching fundamentally decent people trying to go about their lives, as opposed to the usual television set piece of 'cops and robbers'. In writing the scripts he sets up as many '*Downton* conundrums' as possible – dilemmas where it is never clear to the audience whose side to be on. Gareth Neame, the show's executive producer who first suggested to Julian that he should write a series following the lives of all the inhabitants both above stairs and below in a country house, thinks people love the show because it is a period drama with the pace of a soap opera. Whatever its magic ingredient, there is no denying that *Downton* has a special something that appeals to everyone, no matter who they are or where they come from.

In compiling this book of Downton Abbey's best lines of wit and wisdom, I was struck by two things. Firstly, you don't need to know the show or the relationships between the characters to find their quotes either laugh-out-loud funny or dab-an-eye poignant. (Although, I couldn't resist a section just on Violet and Isobel's sparring.) And, secondly, how extraordinary it is that one person should have written all of these lines. There's no team of writers alongside Julian – he sits, quite alone, wherever he finds himself working, whether at his desk in Dorset or on a plane to New York, and taps out hours and hours of scripts, each containing not only plots for a myriad of characters but also these highly quotable lines. I'm not afraid to say that in the re-reading of these scripts, sometimes for the fourth or fifth time, I had tears streaming down my cheeks. There are millions and millions of appreciative *Downton Abbey* viewers across the world, and one very proud niece.

Jessica Fellowes

CHAPTER ONE

Life

LIFE IS . . .

Mrs Patmore: Nothing in life is sure.

Violet: Life is a game in which the player
must appear ridiculous.

Carson: In my opinion, to misquote
Doctor Johnson, if you're tired of style,
you are tired of life.

Mrs Hughes: My advice, Daisy, is to go as far in
life as God and luck allow.

Violet: My dear, all life is a series of problems
which we must try and solve, first one and
then the next and the next, until at last we die.

Carson: The business of life is the acquisition of
memories. In the end that's all there is.

Blake: I loved Rose's definition of
ordinary life: dancing and shopping
and seeing one's friends.

Carson: Hard work and diligence weigh
more than beauty in the real world.
Violet: If only that were true.

ALL THE WORLD'S A STAGE . . .

Violet: Have we all stepped through
the looking glass?

Robert: We all have chapters we would
rather keep unpublished.

IF IT ALL GOES WRONG, YOU ONLY
HAVE YOURSELF TO BLAME . . .

Branson: We all live in a harsh world.
But at least I know I do.

Mrs Hughes: The Big Parade's passed by,
Mr Carson. We're just trying to keep up
as best we can.

Robert: By thinking sensibly,
you mean thinking like you.
Violet: Of course.

Violet: Well, in my experience, second
thoughts are vastly overrated.

HOPE . . .

Bates: Nothing is harder to live
with than false hope.

Mrs Hughes: Where there's life, there's hope.

Jimmy: I have dreams. But they don't
involve peeling potatoes.

Violet: Hope is a tease, designed to
prevent us accepting reality.

Bates: What do they call extreme optimism?
Anna: They call it 'making the best of things'
and that is what we'll do.

Cora: There's nothing more tiring than
waiting for something to happen.

Robert: It's better to know the truth than to
live in a cloud of mystery and despair.

FAITH . . .

Robert: I wouldn't know what to do.
All that crossing and bobbing up and down.
I went to a Mass once in Rome, it was
more like a gymnastic display.

Sinderby: The second Lord Sinderby
may be Jewish, but the third will not. And soon
our family will be one more British dynasty
with all the same prejudices as everyone else
who shops at Harrods!

Violet: Principles are like prayers.
Noble, of course, but awkward at a party.

. . . AND CHARITY

Sybil: It's the gloomy things that need our help.
If everything in the garden is sunny,
why meddle?

Mary: It's easy to be generous when
you have nothing to lose.

Cora: What's the matter, Robert? Are you afraid you'll be converted while you're not looking?

Henry: I never meant it to happen. Isn't there something called Forgiveness Through Good Intention?
Mary: Only for Catholics.

UP WITH THE BRITS!

Robert: British justice! Envy of the world.

Pamuk: Why are you English so curious
about other people's lives?

Rosamund: There's nothing like an
English summer, is there?
Mary: Except an English winter.

Edith: I sometimes feel we should make more
scenes. About things that really matter to us.
Gillingham: It wouldn't be very English.

Violet: Like all Englishmen of his type,
he hid his qualities beneath a thick blanket
of convention, so I didn't see who he
really was at first.

Robert: The English have strong principles,
except when it comes to the chance of good
shooting or eating well.

Harold: Well I thought well-born English girls
were supposed to be reticent and refined.
Madeleine: That was before the war.

ON THE UPPER CLASSES

Violet: A peer in favour of reform is like a
turkey in favour of Christmas.

Edith: Our way of life is something strange,
something people queue up and buy a ticket to
see, a museum exhibit, a fat lady in the circus.

Grigg: You won't always be in charge, you
know. The day is coming when your lot will
have to toe the line, just like the rest of us.

Mary: Women like me don't have a life. We
choose clothes and pay calls and work for charity.

Branson: 'Flattered' is a word posh people use
when they're getting ready to say no.

Branson: You're like all of your kind. You think
you have the monopoly of honour.

Violet: The aristocracy has not survived
by its intransigence.

Mary: Well, I suppose I must accept that in a
post-war world we toffs are the villains of
every story.

Mary: Families like ours are always hunting families.

Violet: The Monarchy has thrived on magic and mystery. Strip them away and people may think the Royal family is just like us.

Violet: It's our job to provide employment. An aristocrat with no servants is as much use to the county as a glass hammer.

Violet: Oh no, if I were to search for logic, I should not look for it among the English upper class.

Mrs Hughes: It seems odd to me that a curtsey and a nod from the Throne can turn you from a girl into a woman. But that's the way they do it, so who are we to argue?

Mary: What will we do about furniture and pictures and everything?
Carlisle: What does anyone do? Buy it, I presume.
Mary: Your lot buys it. My lot inherits it.

Cora: I think accepting change is quite as important as defending the past.

Robert: If we don't respect the past we'll find it harder to build our future.

KNOW YOUR PLACE

Robert: Cheer up, Carson. There are worse
things happening in the world.
Carson: Not worse than a maid serving a duke.

O'Brien: She hasn't even got a lady's maid.
Anna: It's not a capital offence.

Gwen: I'm the daughter of a farmhand.
I'm lucky to be a maid. I was born with
nothing, and I'll die with nothing.

Gwen: You're brought up to think it's all within
your grasp, that if you want something enough it'll come to you.
Well we're not like that. We don't think our dreams are bound to
come true, because they almost never do.

Cora: Robert? A world famous singer is in our house,
a great artist honoured by the King, but you felt it beneath
your dignity to eat with her?
Robert: What does one say to a singer?

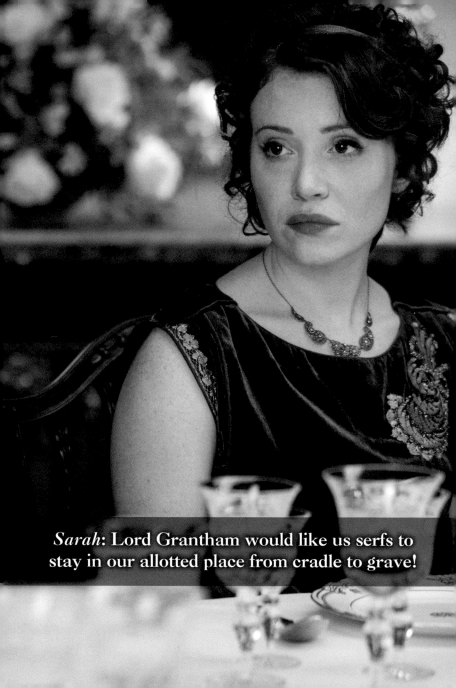

Sarah: Lord Grantham would like us serfs to stay in our allotted place from cradle to grave!

Violet: It is not your place even to have opinions of my acquaintance. Let alone express them.

Carson: You are the Under Butler, a post that is fragrant with the memories of a lost world. No one is sorrier to say it than I am, but you are not a creature of today.

Carson: They respect you, of course. But I'm their leader.
Mrs Hughes: Well, that's put me in my place.
Carson: Don't envy me, Mrs Hughes. You know what they say. Uneasy lies the head that wears the crown.

Isobel: Servants are always far more conservative than their employers. Everyone knows that.

William: Are we to treat him as the heir?
O'Brien: Are we heck as like. A doctor's son from Manchester? He'll be lucky if he gets a civil word out of me.
Anna: We're all lucky if we get a civil word out of you.

Cora: I'm afraid meeting us all together must be very intimidating.
Violet: I do hope so.

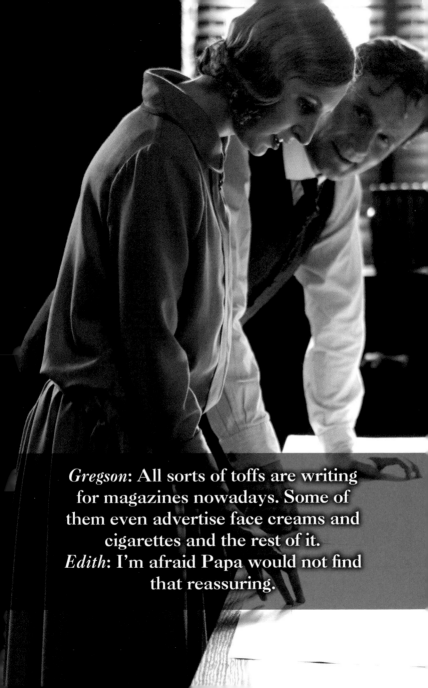

Gregson: All sorts of toffs are writing for magazines nowadays. Some of them even advertise face creams and cigarettes and the rest of it.
Edith: I'm afraid Papa would not find that reassuring.

GOING UP . . . GOING DOWN

Ethel: Why shouldn't she learn how to cook and
scrub? . . . Things are changing.

> *Violet*: I have lived through great wars and
> my share of grief. I think I can manage an
> impertinent question from a doctor.

Violet: I haven't been into the kitchens
here for at least, oh, twenty years at least.
Isobel: Have you brought your passport?

> *Clarkson*: Nurse Crawley, I may not be your
> social superior in a Mayfair ballroom, but in this
> hospital I have the deciding voice.

> *Matthew*: I won't let them change me.
> *Isobel*: Why would they want to?
> *Matthew*: Mother, Lord Grantham has made
> the unwelcome discovery that his heir is a
> middle-class lawyer and the son of a
> middle-class doctor.
> *Isobel*: *Upper* middle class.

IN THE CHANGING WORLD, SOME OF US
ARE NEITHER FISH NOR FOWL . . .

Rose: You live there too, you know.
Branson: I'm not sure where I live. I feel
   sometimes I'm hanging in mid-air –

                Violet: It's time he decided whether he is fish,
                      flesh, fowl or good red herring.

         Branson: I just felt like an intruder.
      It made me face the fact that I'm living
            where I don't belong.
         Edith: Welcome to the club.
          Mary: Oh, stop moaning.

Thomas: Still, it's pathetic for a lady to be
       pining over a footman.
  Jimmy: Excuse me. I think it shows
      very good taste.

           Branson: You won't make a gentleman
        of me, you know. You can teach me to fish, to
         ride and to shoot, but I'll still be an
          Irish Mick in my heart.

Edith: It feels so wild. To be out with a man, drinking and dining in a smart London restaurant. Can you imagine being allowed to do anything of the sort five years ago, never mind ten?

CHANGE

Carson: Life's altered you, as it altered me.
And what would be the point of living if we
didn't let life change us?

Robert: Sometimes I feel like a creature in
the wilds, whose natural habitat is gradually
being destroyed.

Mary: The world moves on
and we must move with it.

Carson: The nature of life is not
permanence but flux.
Mrs Hughes: Just so. Even if it does
sound faintly disgusting.

Mrs Hughes: Perhaps the world is
becoming a kinder place.
Carson: You say 'kinder'. I say weaker
and less disciplined.

Robert: It's a brave new world we're headed for,
no doubt about that. We must try to meet it with
as much grace as we can muster . . .

Branson: Sometimes a hard sacrifice must be
made for a future that's worth having.

Martha: The world has moved
on since we last met.
Carson: And we have moved on with it, madam.
Martha: Really? It seems so strange to think of the
English embracing change.

Violet: It's so encouraging to see
the future unfurl.
Martha: As long as you remember it will bear no
resemblance to the past.

Carson: Why does everyone talk as if we
don't live in the modern world?
Mrs Hughes: You don't agree with that, then?
Carson: No! Does the King not live in the
world of today? Does Mr Sargent not paint
modern pictures? Does Mr Kipling not
write modern books?

Carson: I don't know. Screaming in the
servants' hall, singers chatting to his lordship,
and a footman cooking the dinner. What a
topsy-turvy world we've come to.

Mrs Hughes: I think it's exciting. We're catching
up, Mr Carson. Whether you like it or not,
Downton is catching up with the times we live in.
Carson: That is exactly what I am afraid of.

Violet: What is a 'weekend'?

CLASS ENVY

Carson: You think they must be having a better time. Then you want them not to have a better time. The next thing you know, there's a guillotine in Trafalgar Square.

Thomas: I'm the one that got away.
Ethel: Gives hope to us all.

Violet: I'm very good at mixing. We always danced the first waltz at the Servants' Ball, didn't we, Carson?

Violet: It always happens when you give these little people power. It goes to their heads like strong drink!

Mary: My lot's going down and your lot's coming up. Is that a receipt for a peaceful co-existence?
Blake: I wouldn't put it like that. I'd say I believe in the future, and so could you.

Molesley: Of course, she married beneath her.
Mrs Patmore: And who are you then, a Hapsburg archduke?

THE SHOCK OF THE NEW . . .

Mrs Hughes: An electric toaster. I've given it to myself as a treat. If it's any good, I'm going to suggest getting one for the upstairs breakfasts.
Carson: Is it not enough that we're sheltering a dangerous revolutionary, Mrs Hughes? Could you not have spared me that?

Mrs Patmore: You don't understand. Before too long, her ladyship could run the kitchen with a woman from the village. What with these toasters and mixers and such like, we'd be out of a job.

Gwen: It's electricity, not the devil's handiwork. You'll have to get used to it sooner or later.

Violet: I couldn't have electricity in the house. I wouldn't sleep a wink. All those vapours seeping about.

Violet: First electricity, now telephones. Sometimes I feels as if I must be living in an H. G. Wells novel.

Violet: Is this an instrument of communication or torture?

Evelyn Napier: Is this your first experience
of jazz, Lady Grantham?
Violet: Oh is that what it is? Do you think any of
them know what the others are playing? Hmm?

Daisy: But if it's electric, aren't you worried
it's going to run away with itself and sew
your fingers to the table?

Carlisle: The train was late.
Robert: Welcome to the new world.

Robert: That's because you're American. But
I'm not, and I find the whole idea a kind of
Thief of Life. That people should waste hours
huddled around a wooden box, listening to
someone talking at them, burbling inanities
from somewhere else.

Cora: Mrs Patmore, is there any
aspect of the present day that you can
accept without resistance?
Mrs Patmore: Well m'lady, I wouldn't
mind getting rid of my corset.

Mary: People do such odd things nowadays.
I once met a man who spent his time
importing guinea pigs from Peru.

THE ROOT OF ALL DOWNTON ABBEY

Violet: Oh, good. Let's talk about money.

Carlisle: That's like the rich who say that money doesn't matter. It matters enough when you haven't got it.

Mary: Richard Carlisle is powerful. He's rich and getting richer. He wants to buy a proper house, you know, with an estate. He says after the war the market will be flooded and we can take our pick.
Violet: Oh, and you can dance on the grave of a fallen family.

Jimmy: Of course it was poker. You can't lose a fortune playing Snap.
Molesley: I could.

Violet: A guinea? For a bottle of scent? Did he have a mask and a gun?

Daisy: A penny for your thoughts.
Mrs Patmore: They're worth a great deal more than that, thank you very much.

Anna: Penny for your thoughts.
Bates: You'd pay twice that not to know them.

FIGHT FOR YOUR RIGHTS

Cora: So women's rights begin at home?
I see. Well, I'm all for that.

Thomas: There is such a thing as free speech.
Mrs Hughes: Not when I'm in charge.

Edith: I hope you won't chain yourself to the
railings and end up being force-fed semolina.

Edith: I don't have the vote. I'm not
over thirty and I'm not a householder.
It's ridiculous.

Violet: Is it proper? For a young
woman to be alone in a flat?
Edith: Granny, Adrienne Bolland flew alone over
the Andes Mountains four years ago, and anyway,
I'm not a 'young woman'. I'm staring middle age
in the face.

Branson: I may be a Socialist
but I'm not a lunatic.
Mary: I'm not sure Papa knows the difference.

Sybil: Women must get the vote, mustn't they, Branson? Why does the Prime Minister resist the inevitable?
Branson: Politicians can't often recognise the changes that are inevitable.

———

Ethel: I'm studying, m'lady. These days a working woman must have a skill.
Violet: But you seem to have so many.

Sarah: I don't want you to hate them. Just to realise that you're more than a retainer. I can't bear for you to waste your life propping up a system that's dying.
Branson: Well, it won't die before dinner.

Branson: I was always against any
personal violence, I swear it.
Violet: Oh, so at least we can sleep in our beds.

Mary: What is your main objection to
Mr MacDonald? That the Prime Minister
is the son of a crofter?
Robert: I couldn't care less if he was the son
of Fu Manchu. What worries me is that our
Government is committed to the destruction of
people like us and everything we stand for.

Blake: Mr Lloyd George is more
concerned with feeding the population than
rescuing the aristocracy. That doesn't seem
mean-spirited to me.

Violet: For years I have watched
Governments take control of our lives and
their argument is always the same. Fewer
costs, greater efficiency, but the result is the
same too. Less control by the people, more
control by the State, until the individual's
own wishes count for nothing. That is what I
consider my duty to resist.
Rosamund: By wielding your
unelected power.

EDUCATION, EDUCATION, EDUCATION

Molesley: I believe education's the gate that
   leads to any future worth having.

Mrs Patmore: All the best people were
   rubbish at numbers at school.

Mason: Education is power. Don't forget that. There's no limit
to what you can achieve, if you'll just give a year or two to
mastering those books.

Daisy: I'm studying the Glorious
Revolution of 1688.
Mrs Patmore: Well there'll be a glorious
revolution down here if you don't watch it!

Carson: You're nervous because
you're intelligent, Alfred. Only stupid
people are foolhardy.

Mary: All we were taught was French,
prejudice and dance steps.

Lady Shackleton: How can I present myself as
an expert when I don't know the facts?
Violet: It's never stopped me.

MANNERS ARE EASY AND LIFE IS HARD

Mrs Patmore: We should always be
polite to people who are kind. There's
not much of it about!

Violet: The presence of strangers is our only
guarantee of good behaviour.

Edith: What do you think Eryholme needs?
Violet: Well, if it's like everywhere else, good manners and some decent conversation.

ON WOMEN

Violet: I'm a woman, Mary. I can be as contrary as I choose.

Violet: I do think a woman's place is *eventually* in the home, but I see no harm in her having some fun before she gets there.

Violet: A woman of my age can face reality far better than most men.

ON MEN

Anna: What I see is a good man, m'lady. And
they're not like buses. There won't be another
one along in ten minutes' time

Mary: Well, he's not bad looking and he's still
alive. Which puts him two points ahead of most
men of our generation.

Anna: I've been on at Mr Bates to take
advantage of being in London and get a few
things. The trouble is he does hate shopping.
Mrs Hughes: That must be because he's a man.

Mrs Patmore: There's nothing wrong with a
man who can cook. Some say the best cooks
in the world are men.

Violet: Spratt, I have told you before.
I do not appreciate a man of mystery.
If you have something to say, say it!

Mrs Hughes: I wish men worried about
our feelings a quarter as much as we worry
about theirs.

Violet: He's a man. Men don't have rights.

HOW TO BE HAPPY

Branson: You seem to think that she can only be
happy in some version of Downton Abbey.
When it's obvious that if she wanted that life,
she would not be marrying me.

Robert: Rose, I leave you in charge of fun.
Rose: Oh mission understood, Captain.

Robert: I'm happy Edith is happy. I'm happy
you mean to keep her happy. That is quite
enough happiness to be going on with.

Matthew: I'm dancing a jig. I feel as if
I've swallowed a box of fireworks.

Mabel: I remember my mother telling me, that
in the end, happiness is a matter of choice.
Some people choose to be happy and others
select a course that leads only to frustration and
disappointment.

Branson: A day of racing cars and pigs.
Who could better that?

Edith: No burning ambitions?
Bertie: Not really. I'm always jealous of those chaps who fly the Channel or invent a cure or something. What about you? Are you pining for some unfulfilled dream?
Edith: Not today. Today I feel very happy.

WHEN HAPPINESS
DOESN'T COME EASILY

Anna: What would you like me to get you?
Edith: A different life.

Edith: Sometimes I feel I've been given one
little bit of happiness and that will have to do.

Matthew: I deserve to be unhappy.
So does Mary.
Isobel: Nobody your age deserves that. And if
you are, and you can do something about it and
don't, well, the war's taught you nothing.

Jane: Will you be happy? Really?
Robert: I have no right to be unhappy,
which is almost the same.

Mary: The odd thing is, I feel, for the first time
really, I understand what it is to be happy.
It's just that I know I won't be.

Thomas: It may surprise you to hear it, Mr
Carson, but I've been happy here.
Carson: I am quite surprised to hear that
you have been happy anywhere.

THE FOLLIES OF YOUTH

Robert: No one's sensible at her age. Nor
should they be. That's our role.

Violet: No one can accuse me of being modern,
but even I can see it's not a crime to be young.

Isobel: It's good to do some crazy things
when you're young.
Cora: As long as you survive them.

OLD AGE IS NO PLACE FOR SISSIES

Robert: And to think Taylor's gone off to run a
tea shop. I cannot feel that'll make for a very
restful retirement, can you?
Carson: I would rather be put to death, m'lord.

Cora: I'm afraid Edith will be the one to
care for us in our old age.
Robert: What a ghastly prospect.

Violet: 1920. Is it to be believed? I feel
as old as Methuselah.
Robert: But so much prettier.

WHAT DOESN'T KILL YOU . . .

Mrs Patmore: If you've got a cold, I want
you out of here.

Clarkson: Mrs Crawley tells me
she's recommended nitrate of silver and
tincture of steel.
Violet: Is she making a suit of armour?

Mrs Hughes: Mr Carson, are you all right?
Carson: Why shouldn't I be?
Mrs Hughes: You've never rung the
dressing gong and Mrs Patmore's doing a
soufflé for the first course.
Carson: Oh, my God—

Mrs Patmore: No one told me there'd
be an actual operation . . .
Anna: What did you think? They were just
going to make magic passes over your eyes?

Violet: Wasn't there a masked ball in Paris when
cholera broke out? Half the guests were dead
before they left the ballroom.
Robert: Thank you, Mama. That's
cheered us up no end.

Mary: Can you manage without your stick?
Matthew: You are my stick.

Mrs Patmore: If you must pay money, better to a
doctor than an undertaker.
Mrs Hughes: If that's an example of your bedside manner, Mrs
Patmore, I think I'd sooner face it alone.

———————

Mrs Patmore: Will it hurt?
Mrs Hughes: Since he has to do it whether it
hurts or not, I don't see the point of that question.

Mrs Hughes: Mrs Patmore, will you
please leave the hysteria to me.

Mrs Hughes: It would be so nice if people
would wait to learn if I really am ill before
boxing me up.

DON'T YOU KNOW THERE'S A WAR ON?

Bates: War is on the way.
William: Then we'll have to face it.
As bravely as we can.
Thomas: Thank you, Mr Cannon Fodder.

Bates: Hard to believe the clouds are
gathering on a summer's day like this.

Violet: War makes early risers of us all.

Carson: Keeping up standards is the only
way to show the Germans that they will not
beat us in the end.

Violet: War deals out strange tasks. Remember
your Great-Aunt Roberta . . . She loaded the
guns at Lucknow.

Matthew: War has a way of distinguishing
between the things that matter, and the things
that don't.

Cora: He's just got to let maids serve
in the dining room.
Robert: Quite right. There is a war.
Even Carson has to make sacrifices.

General: We old codgers have our work cut out for us keeping spirits high at home. Someone must.
Robert: Oh, indeed sir.

Isobel: I'm sure he'll have seen worse things at
the front than a dinner with no footmen.

Robert: We've dreamed a dream, my dear, but
now it's over. The world was in a dream before
the war, but now it's woken up and said goodbye
to it. And so must we.

Violet: War breaks down barriers, and when
peacetime re-erects them it's very easy to find
oneself on the wrong side.

Sybil: Sometimes it feels as if all the men I ever
danced with are dead.

Isobel: I don't want my own son to die,
either! But this is a war! And we must be in it
together! High and low, rich and poor! There
can be no 'special cases', because every man at
the front is a special case to someone!

Mary: Didn't the war teach you never
to make promises?

KEEP CALM AND DOWNTON ABBEY

Violet: Ah. Just the ticket. Nanny always said
sweet tea was just the thing for frayed nerves.

> *Edith*: I am a useful spinster, good at helping
> out. That is my role. And spinsters get up for
> breakfast.

> *Violet*: What about me? Where am I to go?
> *Robert*: We still own most of the village.
> *Violet*: Perhaps I could open a shop.

Violet: You are a woman with a brain and
reasonable ability. Stop whining and find
something to do!

Sybil: No one hits the bull's eye
with the first arrow.

> *Violet*: Don't be defeatist, dear.
> It's very middle class.

> *Gwen*: Only a fool doesn't know when
> they've been beaten.
> *Sybil*: Then I'm a fool, for I'm a long way
> from being beaten yet.

Branson: Take an interest in something. Doesn't matter what. Poetry or carpentry, history or hats.

Cora: You are being tested. And do you know what they say, my darling? Being tested only makes you stronger.

Edith: Aren't you being very snobbish?
Violet: We are being realistic, something your generation has such trouble with.

Mrs Patmore: Sympathy butters no parsnips.

Violet: Oh, all this endless 'thinking'. It's very over-rated . . . I blame the war. Before 1914 nobody thought about anything at all.

Mrs Patmore: Oh cheer up, Mr Molesley. It may never happen.
Molesley: It already has.

CHAPTER TWO

Love and Family

Violet: I am not a romantic. But even I will concede that the heart does not exist solely for the purpose of pumping blood.

LOVE IS . . .

Branson: Real love means giving someone
the power to hurt you.

Robert: Are you warm enough?
Cora: I am when you're holding my hand.

Shrimpie: Love is like riding or speaking
French. If you don't learn it young, it's hard to
get the trick of it later.

Mrs Hughes: We must all have our hearts
broken once or twice before we're done.

Violet: My dear, love is a far more dangerous
motive than dislike.

Carson: Well, to be young is to have your
heart broken. In the kitchens at Downton, like
everywhere else.

Violet: I do not speak much of the heart, since
it's seldom helpful to do so, but I know well
enough the pain when it is broken.

Anna: I know what real love is, and there
aren't many who can say that. I'm one of the
lucky ones.

SINGLETONS

Rosamund: Beware of being too good at it.
That's the danger of living alone. It can be very
hard to give up.

Matthew: I am the cat that walks by himself
and all places are alike to me. I have nothing
to give and nothing to share. And if you were
not engaged to be married, I wouldn't let you
anywhere near me.

Daisy: I've never been special to anyone.

Edith: Love and position, in one handsome
package. Who could ask for more?

Mary: I'd rather be alone than
with the wrong man.

Rosamund: After four Seasons, one is less
a debutante than a survivor.

Cora: I'm afraid we're rather a female party
tonight, Duke. But you know what it's like
trying to balance numbers in the country. A
single man outranks the Holy Grail.

Mrs Patmore: **Sometimes you can spend too long on a one-sided love.**

———————

Robert: Mary has more suitors tonight than the Princess Aurora.

Rose: What's a group noun for suitors?
Cora: What do you think? A desire?
Rosamund: A Desire of Suitors. Very good.
Mary: If you're going to talk nonsense, I have better things to do.

Mrs Hughes: A broken heart can be as painful as a broken limb.

Mrs Hughes: You can always hold my hand if you
need to feel steady.
Carson: I don't know how, but you manage to
make that sound a little risqué.

LESSONS IN FLIRTING

Blake: By the time we got back, we looked
as if we'd been wrestling in mud.
Gillingham: And had you?
Mary: No. But then it's always nice to leave
something for another time.

Molesley: It's just coffee. You won't have to
surrender any of your independence.

Blake: I find – perhaps to my surprise – that,
since I left, I can't think of anything but you.

Mrs Hughes: You're very flattering. When you
talk like that, you make me want to check the
looking glass to see that my hair's tidy.
Carson: Get away with you.

William: Pinch me.
I am your dream come true.

Kemal: Sometimes we must endure a little
pain in order to achieve satisfaction.

Violet: You flatter me,
which is just as it should be.

Matthew: If you really like an argument –
Mary: Yes?
Matthew: We should see more of each other.

THERE'S A TIME AND PLACE FOR EVERYTHING, EVEN COMPLIMENTS . . .

Daisy: Upset? Mrs Patmore, if you knew what it feels like to have a young man keen to court me. I'd kiss him if it wouldn't give him the wrong idea. Upset? I'm that chuffed it'll take me through to next summer.

Mrs Patmore: No man's wanted to squire me since the Golden Jubilee. Even then he expected me to buy the drinks.

Bricker: Please. You said yourself she wouldn't mind and as for your clothes, you'll be the best-looking woman in the Ritz dining room, whatever you're wearing.
Cora: Golly. That's cheered me up.

Mrs Patmore: It's a long time since anyone wanted to share my seat on the bus, never mind my heart and home.

KISSES

Sybil: Yes, you can kiss me, but that is all
until everything is settled.
Branson: For now, God knows it's enough
that I can kiss you.

Anna: I'd give you a smack if I didn't want
to kiss you so much I could burst!

Gregson: What, here? In front of
all these people?
Edith: I don't care. Kiss me. Now.

Gillingham: Will you kiss me? Please. I will
never love again as I love you in this moment.
And I must have something to remember.

PLAYING WITH FIRE

Robert: I want you with every fibre of my being.
But it isn't fair to you, it isn't fair to anyone.

Violet: Seriously, my dear, you have to
take control of your feelings, before they take
control of you.

Mary: It was lust, Matthew, or a need for
excitement or something in him that I – Oh,
God, what difference does it make? I'm Tess
of the d'Urbervilles to your Angel Clare. I have
fallen. I am impure.

Edith: It reminds me of Lady Warwick having
the stable bell at Easton rung at six, so everyone
had to time to get back to the right beds before
their maids and valets arrived.

Mary: Are we talking about sex? Or love?
Blake: Oh that is a question that mankind has
been wrestling with since the dawn of time.
Good night.

Mrs Patmore: Well, there's nothing so
terrible about it, is there? So they say. I wouldn't
know, of course.

TRYING IT ON

Mrs Hughes: What's he done? That all young
men aren't anxious to do, behind the bicycle
sheds every night?

Carson: Going on? Nothing 'goes on' in any
house where I'm in authority.

Mrs Hughes: He didn't hurt you?
Ivy: No. But he asked for things no man
should want before they're married.
Mrs Patmore: Yes, I think we're a bit more
clear about that than they are.

Jimmy: Oh come on. I only asked what
a million men would ask.
Ivy: And I only answered what a million
women would answer.

Violet: He just wants what all men want.
Isobel: Oh don't be ridiculous!
Violet: I was referring to companionship.
As I hope you were.

Mrs Patmore: Mr Carson, all women
need someone to show a bit of interest every
now and then, preferably in a manner that's
not entirely proper.

Ivy: I s'pose he's been sweet-talking me so he could have his way. And all this time I thought he was so nice.
Mrs Patmore: I wonder how many women have said that since the Norman Conquest.

A REPUTATION RUINED

Cora: When you refused Matthew, you were
the daughter of an earl with an unsullied
reputation. Now you are damaged goods.

Violet: In my day, a lady was incapable of feeling
physical attraction until she'd been instructed
to do so by her Mama.

Susan: She looks like a slut.
Violet: Heavens. That's not a word you often
hear among the heather.

FORBIDDEN LOVE

Rose: You mustn't be so self-conscious.
Jack Ross: A black singer with the daughter of a
marquess in a north Yorkshire town. Why should
we attract any attention?

Robert: If I'd shouted blue murder every
time someone tried to kiss me at Eton, I'd
have gone hoarse in a month.

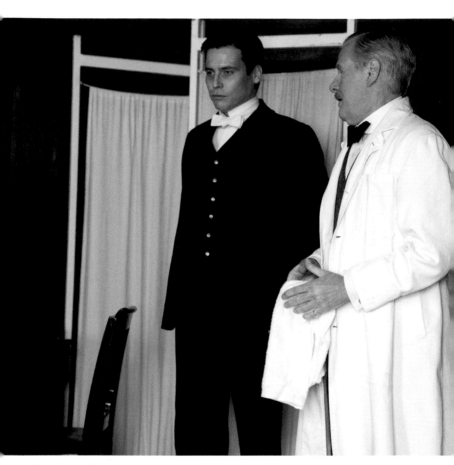

Clarkson: My advice to you, Thomas, would be to accept the burden that chance has seen fit to lay upon you, and to fashion as good a life as you are able. Remember: Harsh reality is always better than false hope.

ARE YOU READY FOR LOVE?

Branson: You won't mind burning your bridges?
Sybil: Mind? Fetch me the matches!

Rose: I mean it. You all think that now I'm
officially 'out' and everything, it's time to find
my man. But I'm only going to marry if I'm
totally, absolutely, in love.

Violet: We'd better get her settled before the
bloom is quite gone off the rose.

Evelyn Napier: A woman who finds me boring
could never love me, and I believe marriage
should be based on love. At least at the start.

Mary: How many times am I to be ordered to
marry the man sitting next to me at dinner?

Mrs Patmore: You don't have to marry him when
it comes to it, but you can't let him go to war
with a broken heart, or he won't come back.

Mary: I'd never marry any man that I was told
to. I'm stubborn. I wish I wasn't, but I am.

Violet: You can normally find an Italian who
isn't too picky.

Mrs Patmore: The more he said about how he liked his beef roasted and his eggs fried and his pancakes flipped, the more I wondered how to get away.

———————

Rosamund: Oh, come along, Mary, be sensible. Can you really see yourself dawdling your life away as the wife of a country solicitor?

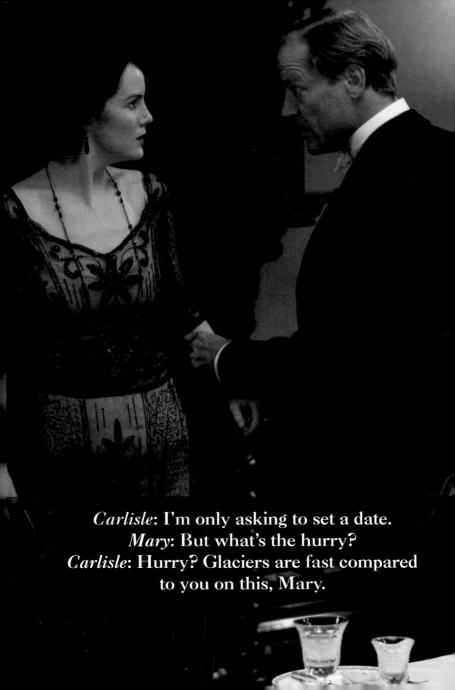

Carlisle: I'm only asking to set a date.
Mary: But what's the hurry?
Carlisle: Hurry? Glaciers are fast compared to you on this, Mary.

PASSIONATE DECLARATIONS

Anna: I love you, Mr Bates. I know it's not ladylike to say it, but I'm not a lady and I don't pretend to be.
Bates: You're a lady to me. And I never knew a finer one.

Merton: I love you, Isobel Crawley. I know it's not enough. I know I'm old and played out. But I do love you with my whole heart.

Matthew: Well, I have to take one thing for granted. That I will love you until the last breath leaves my body.
Mary: Oh, my darling. Me too, me too.

Anna: I've let you down.
Bates: There are no words less true than those. You could never let me down.

Lavinia: I love you. I'm going to look after you. That's all there is to it.

Mary: Did you love Bates more than anyone else in the world?
Anna: I did. I do. I'll never love again like I love him. Never.

Kuragin: I wanted you from the moment I first saw you. More than mortal man ever wanted woman.

Bates: You are not spoiled. You are made higher to me, and holier, because of the suffering you have been put through. You are my wife, and I have never been prouder, nor loved you more than I love you now, at this moment.

Carson: I love her, Mrs Patmore. I am happy and tickled and bursting with pride that she would agree to be my wife, and I want us to live as closely as two people can, for the time that remains to us on earth.

DOWN ON ONE KNEE . . .

Carlisle: Oh, I can talk about love and moon and June and all the rest of it, if you wish. But we're more than that. We're strong and sharp, and we can build something worth having, you and I, if you'll let us.
Mary: Your proposal is improving by leaps and bounds.

Cora: I hope you thanked Matthew properly.
Mary: I got them to make him some sandwiches.
Cora: That's not quite what I meant.
Mary: And he asked me to marry him.
Cora: Heavens! What did they put in them?

Mary: I assume you're going to give me an explanation at some stage?
Gillingham: It's not complicated. I have made a long journey to ask a short question. Will you marry me?

Merton: My proposal is a romantic one. I state freely and proudly, Isobel, that I have fallen in love with you. And I want to spend what remains of my life in your company. I believe I could make you happy. At any rate, I, I should very much like the chance to try.

Isobel: When I got engaged, I was so in love with
Reginald, I felt sick. I was sick with love. Literally.
It seems so odd to think about it now, it really does.
Branson: It was the same for me; as if I'd gone mad
or been hypnotised or something. For days, weeks,
all I could think about was her.
Mary: And me. I was standing outside in the snow
and I didn't have a coat, but I wasn't cold, because
all I kept thinking was: 'He's going to propose, he's
going to propose . . .'
Isobel: Well. Aren't we the lucky ones?

Matthew: I think this is black and white. Do
you love me enough to spend your life with me?
If you don't, then say no. If you do, then say yes.

Branson: I promise to devote every waking
minute to your happiness.

Carson: I do want to be stuck with you.
Mrs Hughes: I'm not convinced I can
be hearing this right.
Carson: You are if you think I'm asking
you to marry me.

Anna: Mr Bates, is this a proposal?
Bates: If that's what you want to call it. And
you might start calling me John.

Violet: No bride should look tired at her wedding.
It either means she's anxious or been up to no good.

BRIDEZILLAS

Cora: Mary was never going to marry on the cheap.
Robert: Oh, no. Nothing must be done on the cheap.

Martha: Dearest Mary. Now you tell me all of
your wedding plans and I'll see what I can do
to improve them.

Martha: Nothing ever alters for you people,
does it? Revolutions erupt and monarchies
crash to the ground, and the groom still cannot
see the bride before the wedding.

Mrs Hughes: But I am the bride! We'll be
doing it your way for the next thirty years –
I know that well enough – but the wedding
day is mine!

Mrs Patmore: That doesn't sound like a bride on
the brink of wedded bliss.
Mrs Hughes: It's a long time since I was on the
brink of anything. Except possibly the grave.

O'Brien: Jilted at the altar. I don't think
I could stand the shame.
Thomas: Then it's lucky no one's ever
asked you, isn't it?

HONEYMOONS

Mary: Smuggle Bates in here when everyone
has gone to bed. And for heaven's sake, make
sure he gets the right room.

Matthew: I'm looking forward to
all sorts of things.
Mary: Don't make me blush.

Edith: I won't sleep a wink.
Sybil: Tonight or tomorrow?
Violet: Sybil, vulgarity is no substitute for wit.

MARRIED LIFE

Violet: One way or another, everyone goes down
the aisle with half the story hidden.

Bates: It's not right for you to cry alone.
You're married and that means you don't
ever have to cry alone again.

Violet: There can be too much truth in
any relationship.

Violet: I never take sides in a broken marriage . . .
Because however much the couple may strive to be honest,
no one is ever in possession of the facts.

Robert: There is no such thing as a marriage
between two intelligent people that does not
sometimes have to negotiate thin ice.

> ***Lady Anstruther***: That's the advantage of an
> older husband. One gets an early release.

Kuragin: You think to be unhappy in a
marriage is ill-bred.
Violet: You do know me, Igor.
That I must concede.

Isobel: Is divorce so very terrible these days? Is it worse to stay together and be miserable?
Sinderby: Well I am clearly old-fashioned, but to me, divorce signifies weakness, degradation, scandal and failure.

Robert: You can't expect me to avoid talking to my own wife.
Violet: Why not? I know several couples who are perfectly content, and haven't spoken for years.

KEEP IT IN THE FAMILY

Robert: If you mistreat her, I will personally have you torn to pieces by wild dogs.
Branson: I'd expect no less.

Violet: Are you glad you came? I mean these are your people now. You must remember that. This is your family.
Branson: This may be my family, but these are not quite my people.

Violet: The one thing we don't want is a poet in the family.

ON PARENTING

Robert: I love my children equally.
Edith: I don't know why people say that, when
it's almost never true.

Violet: Poor souls. It's bad enough parenting a
child when you like each other.

THE SECRETS OF DOWNTON ABBEY

Cora: I hate to lie.
Mary: I'll do it. I don't mind lying.

Clarkson: Even to ease suffering, I could never
justify telling an outright lie.
Violet: Have we nothing in common?

Violet: We both know you are not leaving my
house until I learn the truth. So, shall I have a
bed made up for you here or are you going to
tell me now?

Carson: All we want to know is what Gwen wants
with a typewriter and why she feels the need to
keep it secret.
Anna: She wants to keep it private, not secret.
There's a difference.

FEUDING IN THE FAMILY

Violet: When we unleash the dogs of war,
we must go where they take us.

Bates: Now, you listen, you filthy little rat. If
you don't lay off, I will punch your shining
teeth through the back of your head.

Cora: Next time you want to treat me like a naughty
schoolgirl, you might do it in private, not in front
of the servants.

Mary: So I must brave the storm?
Matthew: You're strong. A storm-braver
if ever I saw one.

Carlisle: I'm leaving in the morning, Lady
Grantham. I doubt we'll meet again.
Violet: Do you promise?

Bricker: Goodness. Is this what they call a
lively exchange of views?
Mary: It's about now that Papa usually
fetches his gun.

Violet: If you were talking in Urdu,
I could not understand you less.

AFTER THE BLOODSHED

Violet: Now if you can all put your swords
away, perhaps we can finish our dinner in a
civilised manner.

O'Brien: Oh, get back in the knife box,
Miss Sharp.

Daisy: I feel so . . . I don't know, dazed.
Yesterday I thought I hated her and today she's
saved our lives.
Mrs Patmore: It never does good to hate anyone.

Denker: Oh, dear. I do hope I haven't cast
a shadow.
Mrs Patmore: What did you think you were
doing? Sprinkling sunshine?

Crowborough: Why did you apologise to that
man? It's not his business what we do.
Mary: I always apologise when I'm in the wrong.
It's a habit of mine.

Matthew: Sorry about the vase.
Violet: Oh, don't be, don't be. It was a wedding
present from a frightful aunt. I have hated it
for half a century.

ON DEATH

Carson: What does it matter anyway?
We shout and scream and wail and cry, but in the
end we must all die.
Mrs Hughes: Well, that's cheered me up.

Violet: No Englishman would dream of
dying in someone else's house. Especially
someone they didn't even know.

Violet: I confess I do not know if I would have
had the strength, mentally or physically, to carry
a corpse the length of this house. But I hope I
would have done.

Mrs Patmore: Nothing makes you hungrier
or more tired than grief. When my sister died,
God rest her soul, I ate my way through four
platefuls of sandwiches at one sitting and slept
round the clock.

Isobel: I have this feeling that when I laugh
or read a book or hum a tune, it means that
I've forgotten him. Just for a moment.
And it's that, that I can't bear.

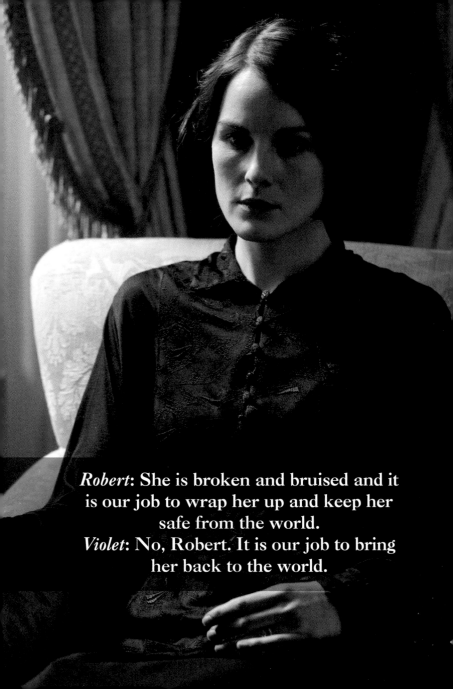

Robert: She is broken and bruised and it is our job to wrap her up and keep her safe from the world.
Violet: No, Robert. It is our job to bring her back to the world.

CHAPTER THREE

Work

ABOVE STAIRS . . .

Mary: Sometimes I rather envy you, having
somewhere to go every morning.

Cora: I can't see why he has a right to your
estate or my money. But I refuse to condemn
him for wanting an honest job.

Violet: There must be something you can
put your mind to.
Edith: Like what? Gardening?
Violet: Well, no. You can't be as desperate as that.

Edith: Listen, everyone. You have a
journalist in the family.
Violet: Since we have a country solicitor and a
car mechanic, it was only a matter of time.

Matthew: Edith has had an invitation to write a
newspaper column.
Violet: And when may she expect an offer to
appear on the London stage?
Edith: See?

Violet: I should far prefer to be a maid in a large
and pleasant house, than work from dawn 'til
dusk in a cramped and gloomy office.

Isobel: Of course, it would be foolish to accuse you of being unprofessional, since you've never had a profession in your life.

***

Sybil: There's nothing wrong with doctors.
We all need doctors.
Mary: We all need crossing sweepers and draymen, too. It doesn't mean we have to dine with them.

Sybil: I know what it is to work now. To have a full day. To be tired in a good way. I don't want to start dress fittings. Or paying calls. Or standing behind the guns.

AND BELOW . . .

Carson: I let myself get flustered. I regard that as highly unprofessional. It won't happen again.

Mrs Patmore: I had to get out of that kitchen if I'm not to be found dead under the table. It's like cooking a banquet three times a day.

O'Brien: We're all essential. Until we get sacked.

Daisy: No farmer is his own boss. He takes his orders from the sun and the snow and the wind and the rain.

O'Brien: It's a hard ladder for a man. For every Escoffier or Monsieur Carême, there's a thousand dogsbodies taking orders from a cross and red-faced old woman.
Mrs Patmore: Who's this you're discussing?

Tim Drewe: Work's like old age, m'lady. The worst thing in the world except for the alternative.

Daisy: What difference does it make if you peel potatoes in London or peel them in Yorkshire?

HOW TO MANAGE THE SERVANTS . . .

Carlisle: I've put in a condition so the builders
are fined for every day they go over.
Violet: Does that make for a happy atmosphere?
Carlisle: I want it done. They can be happy
in their own time.

Anna: What is the first law of service? We do not
discuss the business of this house with strangers!

Mrs Hughes: There are rules to this way of life, Edna.
And if you're not prepared to live by them, then it's not
the right life for you.

Carson: I'm sure the chain of command
will be sorted out soon.
O'Brien: Or there'll be blood on the stairs.

Carson: No footman should be over
six foot one.

Isobel: Servants are human beings, too.
Violet: Yes. But preferably only on their days off.

Molesley: I'll do this, he says, and I'll take the
other, I'll tie that. And I'm just stood there like
a chump watching a man get dressed.

Jimmy: But her ladyship said we
were to enjoy ourselves.
Carson: Let us consider this. She wants you to
enjoy yourself, I want you to run the tent. Now,
which of us can make your life more uncomfortable?

QUEEN OF THE KITCHEN

Mrs Patmore: Leave it, Daisy! He's a grown
man. I suppose he can lift a meat pie.

Mrs Patmore: Get those kidneys up to the
servery before I knock you down and serve
your brains as fritters.

Mrs Patmore: Daisy? What's happened? I said
you could go for a drink of water,
not a trip up the Nile.

Daisy: I was only trying to help.
Mrs Patmore: Oh, like Judas was only 'trying
to help' I s'pose, when he brought the
Roman soldiers to the gardens!

Daisy: I think I've let misself down.
Mrs Patmore: It can't be a new sensation.

Mrs Patmore: Go and grate that suet
before I grow old and die.

Mrs Patmore: You couldn't be harder
on those potatoes if you wanted them to
confess to spying.

SOMETIMES YOU JUST CAN'T
GET THE STAFF

Violet: I was right about my maid. She's leaving –
to get married. How can she be so selfish?

Isobel: It seems rather unlikely to think of
Spratt with a private life.
Violet: Hmm, yes, unlikely and extremely
inconvenient.

Violet: Do we think she's mad? Ill?
Or working for the Russians?

Robert: Are we living under a curse? Doomed
to lose our lady's maids at regular intervals?

Carson: Mr Molesley, I am glad you are, as
you put it, 'willing'. But I cannot feel the word
expresses the kind of enthusiasm I'm looking
for in a new footman.

Robert: You know there is nothing more
ill-bred than to steal other people's servants?

Isobel: I think Cousin Robert is referring to
Ethel's work as a prostitute.
Violet: Well, of course, these days servants
are very hard to find.

Carson: We are about to host a Society wedding. I have no time for training young hobbledehoys.

Ethan: Would you care for one of these? I think they're quite nice.
Carson: You're a footman, not a travelling salesman. Please keep your opinions on the catering to yourself!

Violet: I know nothing of Spratt's friends. I know he certainly has a great many relations, who seem to be married and buried with numbing regularity. Usually on very inconvenient dates.

THERE ARE SOME THINGS A SERVANT JUST WILL NOT DO

Carson: I am not dressing a chauffeur.

Daisy: I'll go to bed when I'm ready.
Mrs Patmore: What's happened to you? Have you swapped places with your evil twin?

Thomas: Mr Carson, must I remind you that I am the Under butler?
Carson: I don't care if you're the High Cockleorum. You're a footman tonight.

Molesley: Now that Jimmy, er James,
has gone, do I take it that I am now
First Footman?
Carson: Since you are the only footman,
you are first, second, third and last! Make what
you will of it!

Daisy: I want to be grown up, Mrs Patmore.
I want responsibility. I want to be an adult. I
can't just stand here, following orders, for the
rest of my life.

A LADY'S MAID HAS MANY
VALUABLE QUALITIES

Anna: Do you want me to answer truthfully
or like a lady's maid?

Violet: Like all lady's maids,
she lives for intrigue.

Mrs Hughes: Really Miss Denker. And in
front of the maids, too.
Denker: Well, who gives a tinker's curse
about the maids?

Violet: I know I'm late. It couldn't be helped. Cora insisted I come without a maid. I can't believe she understood the implications.

Robert: I don't know why you're making such a fuss, Mama. You'd visit Denker if she were locked up.
Violet: Only to check if the locks were sound.

'HOW TO COOK' BY MRS PATMORE

Mrs Patmore: Fold it in, don't slap it! You're making a cake, not beating a carpet!

Mrs Patmore: Oh, talk about making a silk purse out of a sow's ear. I wish we had a sow's ear. It'd be better than this brisket.

Mrs Patmore: Oh not those bowls, Ivy! Chilled soup should be an exquisite mouthful, not a bucket of slop!

Mrs Patmore: Anyone who has the use of their limbs can make a salmon mousse.

Daisy: Alfred's making the sauces for dinner and
Mrs Patmore's having a heart attack.
Carson: I'm not surprised.
Daisy: No, I mean really!

CHAPTER FOUR

Play

EVERYTHING TO EXCESS

Violet: All this unbridled joy has given me
quite an appetite.

Anna: Dinner, supper and no doubt a big
breakfast tomorrow. It's a wonder they're not
all the size of a tub.

Violet: If the poor don't want it,
you can bring it over to me.

Anna: Mr Carson likes to serve two white wines,
which you should open and decant just before
they eat. A light one for the hors d'oeuvres, then
a heavier one with the soup. Keep that going
for the fish and then change to claret, which you
should really decant now. There's a pudding
wine and, after that, whatever they want in the
drawing room with their coffee.
Molesley: Blimey. It's a wonder they make
it up the stairs.

Robert: They do say there's a wild man
inside all of us.
Violet: If only he would stay inside.

FRIENDSHIP AND THE
COUNTESS DOWAGER

Violet: An unlucky friend is tiresome enough,
an unlucky acquaintance is intolerable.

Cora: Are we to be friends, then?
Violet: We are allies, my dear. Which can be
a good deal more effective.

Violet: I don't dislike him. I just don't like him,
which is quite different.

Violet: There's nothing simpler than avoiding
people you don't like. Avoiding one's friends,
that's the real test.

Violet: If I withdrew my friendship from
everyone who had spoken ill of me, my
address book would be empty.

FUN AND GAMES

Cora: You know Rosamund wants to take
you to the theatre.
Violet: Oh I don't think so. Oh no, I'm too tired
for an evening of second-hand emotion.

Violet: A card game? Here? What are the
ladies supposed to do? Put feathers in their
hair and light the gentlemen's cigars?

Rose: I love cocktail parties.
Cora: Me too. You only have to stay forty
minutes, instead of sitting for seven courses,
between a deaf landowner and an even deafer
major general.

Violet: The combination of open air picnics and
after-dinner poker make me feel as though
I've fallen through a looking glass into the
déjeuner sur l'Herbe.

Violet: I'm exhausted. Two parties in
one day is too much for me.

Molesley: You see how my grip is firm but tender.
Cherish the ball, don't crush it.

WHAT TO WEAR

Sybil: Golly, my corset's tight. Anna, when
you've done that, could you be an angel
and loosen it a bit?
Edith: The start of the slippery slope.
Sybil: I'm not putting on weight.
Edith: It didn't shrink in the drawer.

Isobel: I like the new fashions. Shorter skirts,
looser cuts. The old clothes were all very well
if one spent the day on a chaise longue, but
if one wants to get anything done, the new
clothes are much better.
Violet: I'll stick to the chaise longue.

Mrs Hughes: I'm too old to think a new
dress will solve anything much.

Violet: In my time I wore the crinoline, the
bustle and the leg-of-mutton sleeve.

Mary: Granny? What do you think?
Violet: Oh, it is you. I thought it was a man
wearing your clothes.

Sybil: Is there anything more thrilling than a new frock?

Mrs Hughes: Tea gowns? We're not in
the 1890s now, Mr Molesley.
Carson: More's the pity . . .

Sarah: The Rule of the Gong. It sounds
like life in a religious order.

Robert: I nearly came down in a dinner
jacket tonight.
Violet: Really? Well, why not a dressing gown?
Or better still, pyjamas?

Carson: Alfred has embarrassed the
family. He forced Mr Crawley to appear
downstairs improperly dressed.
O'Brien: Oh, you make it sound
quite exciting.

Violet [to Robert]: Oh, I'm so sorry,
I thought you were a waiter.

Branson: I know it's meant to be kind, but I
can think of better ways to help the
needy than sending stiff
collars to the equator.

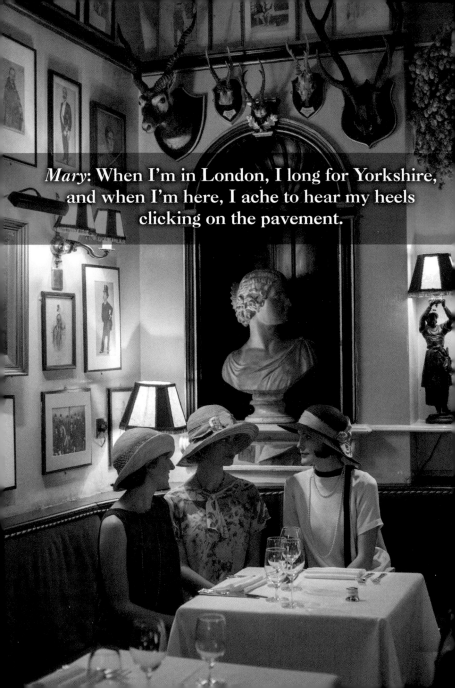

Mary: When I'm in London, I long for Yorkshire, and when I'm here, I ache to hear my heels clicking on the pavement.

LONDON LIFE

Mrs Hughes: How was London?
Carson: Much as usual. Dirty, noisy and
quite enjoyable.

Edith: People aren't so curious in London.
Rosamund: No. They couldn't care less.

Mrs Hughes: I'm happy to tell you that
most things you can buy in Ripon are also
available in London.
Mrs Patmore: I know, but you don't trust
them quite the same, do you?

Violet: My dear, we country-dwellers
must beware of being provincial. Try and
let your time in London rub off on you
a little more.

HUNTIN', SHOOTIN', FISHIN' . . .

Violet: Perhaps he's heard enough
banging for one life.

Carson: Maids at a shooting lunch? Hardly.

Nield: Now, take your time. You're not chasing
a pheasant. Be calm and confident. These
are noble beasts. We must take them out for
the good of the herd, but they've earned our
respect and they deserve a clean death.

Nield: His lordship was born with a rod in
one hand and a gun in the other.
Shrimpie: That sounds rather uncomfortable.

Violet: That is the thing about nature.
There's so much of it.

Mary: I never know which is worse:
the sorrow when you hit the bird,
or the shame when you miss it.

OUR AMERICAN COUSINS

Cora: I hope I don't hear sounds
of disagreement.
Violet: Is that what they call discussion
in New York?

Cora: I might send her over to visit my aunt.
She could get to know New York.
Violet: Oh, I don't think things are
quite that desperate.

Cora: Things are different in America –
Violet: I know. They live in wigwams.

Cora: I'm an American. I don't share your
English hatred of comfort.

Cora: Don't worry about me. I'm an American.
Have gun, will travel.

Mrs Patmore: She ate it, then. I'm never sure
about Americans and offal.

Reed: I'm an American, Alfred, and this is 1920.
Time to live a little.

Violet: You Americans never understand the importance of tradition –
Martha: Yes, we do. We just don't give it power over us. History and tradition took Europe into a world war. Maybe you should think about letting go of its hand.

Robert: You do know the Americans have a correct uniform for practically every activity known to man?

Martha: Oh, well, the gang's all here, I see.
Violet: Is that American for 'Hello'?

THEY DO THINGS DIFFERENTLY THERE . . .

Carson: I always think there's something rather foreign about high spirits at breakfast.

Mrs Hughes: There seems to be a good deal of emotion being vented among the guests in the library. But then they are foreigners.

Violet: Rosamund has no interest in French. If she wishes to be understood by a foreigner, she shouts.

Violet: My husband was a great traveller, so I have spent many happy evenings without understanding a word. The thing is to keep smiling and never look as if you disapprove.

Susan: It'll be filthy and dirty and the food will be awful and there'll be no one to talk to within a hundred square miles.
Violet: That sounds like a week with my mother-in-law.

Mrs Patmore: I don't think we need praise from the French quite yet.

Violet: Switzerland has everything to offer, except perhaps conversation and one can learn to live without that.

Edith: I envy it. All those Latins screaming and shouting and hurling themselves into graves. I bet they feel much better afterwards.
Mary: I wonder. I think once you've let it out, it must be hard to get it back in.

CHAPTER FIVE

Downton Abbey

Martha: Come war and peace, Downton still stands and the Crawleys are still in it.

Branson: It is a bit wild. Jazz at Downton Abbey.

Robert: You see a million bricks that may crumble, a thousand gutters and pipes that may block and leak, and stone that will crack in the frost . . . I see my life's work.

Violet: God knows who the next heir will be. Probably a chimney sweep from Solihull.

Branson: Every man or woman who marries into this house, every child born into it, has to put their gifts at the family's disposal.

Carson: Downton is a great house, Mr Bates, and the Crawleys are a great family. We live by certain standards and those standards can at first seem daunting.

Violet: You'll find there's never a dull moment in this house.

Violet: It's like living in a second-rate hotel where the guests keep arriving and no one seems to leave.

Mary: We need to build something that will last, Papa. Not stand by and watch it crumble into dust.

THE SPARRING PARTNERS

Violet: You are quite wonderful the way you see
room for improvement wherever you look. I
never knew such reforming zeal.
Isobel: I take that as a compliment.
Violet: I must have said it wrong.

Isobel: Cousin Violet is in part to blame.
Violet: Yes, I usually am.

Isobel: How you hate to be wrong!
Violet: I wouldn't know. I'm not familiar
with the sensation.

Isobel: It's only me.
Violet: I always feel that greeting betrays
such a lack of self-worth.

Isobel: Fear not. I have never travelled with
a maid, you can share my knowledge of the
jungle.
Violet: Can't you even offer help without
sounding like a trumpeter on the peak of the
moral high ground?

Isobel: What should we call each other?
Violet: We could always start with Mrs Crawley
and Lady Grantham.

———

Isobel: Say what you like. But I know you care
about these things as much as I do.
Violet: Oh! Nobody cares about anything as
much as you do.

Isobel [to Violet]: It's a nut cracker. We
thought you'd like it. To crack your nuts.

Violet: Oh Robert, it is not a matter of what she
likes. It is her fuel. Some people run on greed,
lust, even love. She runs on indignation!

Isobel: How are we today?
Violet: My dear, please stop talking to me
as if I were a child past hope.

Isobel: I'm a feeble substitute for the
entire Crawley family.
Violet: Hmm, yes, but you're better
than nothing.
Isobel: How warming you make that sound.

Violet: She brought a book with her. That
should keep her occupied.
Robert: What sort of book?
Violet: I can only tell you that, on the train,
it was far more interesting than me.

Isobel: No, no, I prefer it. I've ridden in the
front seat many times.
Violet: Aren't you a wild thing?

Isobel: Cousin Violet has never let a matter of
convenience stand in the way of a principle.
Violet: As the kettle said to the pot.

Isobel: You and I differ when it comes
to the importance of things.
Violet: Does it ever get cold on the
moral high ground?

Isobel: Oh you only say that to sound clever.
Violet: I know. You should try it.

Edith: I suppose Cousin Isobel is entitled
to put up an argument.
Violet: Of course she is. She is just not
entitled to win it.

Isobel: You'll stop at nothing to get your way.
Isn't that the truth?
Violet: Indeed. It is a quality I share with
Marlborough, Wellington and my late mother.
I've trained in a hard school and I fight
accordingly.

AND YET – CAN'T LIVE WITH EACH OTHER, CAN'T LIVE WITHOUT . . .

Violet: Isobel and I had a lot in
common and I shall miss that.
Mary: Granny, you're quite dewy-eyed.
I never think of you as sentimental.
Violet: Nor am I. You've made me regret my
confidence. Do have some cake. And for your
information, I don't think Isobel has ever
looked up to me.

Violet: Uhum. She is a good woman, and while the phrase is enough to set one's teeth on edge, there are moments when her virtue demands admiration.

IF ISOBEL'S NOT AROUND, THERE'S ALWAYS MARTHA TO PLAY WITH

Violet: It is marvellous the way our families support each other.
Martha: You mean you needed the Levinson cash to keep the Crawleys on top.

Martha: I have no wish to be a Great Lady.
Violet: No, a decision that must be reinforced whenever you look in the glass.
Martha: I don't mind looking in the mirror. Because what I see is a woman who's not afraid of the future. My world is coming nearer and your world? It's slipping further and further away. Good night.

ON ANNA

Baxter: What about Mrs Bates? Is she an
enemy? She knows what's going on.
Thomas: No, she's not an enemy. But she's
incorruptible, so we have nothing in common.

Anna: Why are you smiling?
Bates: Because whenever I see a problem,
you see only possibilities.

ON BRANSON

Violet: I'm afraid Tom's small talk
is very small indeed.
Robert: Not everyone can be Oscar Wilde.
Violet: What a relief.

Robert: Tom is our tame revolutionary.
Strallan: Every family should have one.

Robert: I wish Tom had arrived.
Cora: It's so nice to hear you say that.
Robert: No, I mean he's bringing Isis
and I do miss her.

Violet: I know he's housebroken, more or less,
but I don't want freedom to go to his head.

ON CARSON

William: I bet he comes from a line of butlers
that goes back to the Conquerors.

Bates: He learned his business and
so will you. Even Mr Carson wasn't born
standing to attention.
Thomas: I hope not for his mother's sake.

Thomas: Imagine Carson without a footman!
Like a ringmaster without a pony.

Mary: He thinks I should say what I really feel.
Anna: Sounds a bit wild for Carson.

Carson: Oh, I am speechless.
Mrs Hughes: I would guess he won't
stay speechless for long.

ON EDITH

Cora: You mustn't be unkind to Edith. She
has fewer advantages than you.
Mary: Fewer? She has none at all.

Violet: Edith, you are a lady,
not Toad of Toad Hall.

Mary: Honestly, Papa. Edith's about
as mysterious as a bucket.

Edith: No. I won't be the County Failure.
Poor demented Lady Edith, who lost her
virtue and her reason.

Edith: Poor Mary. She hates to be left
behind when everyone else is getting on
with their lives.
Mary: It isn't that. It's the thought of
being left behind with you.

ON MARY

Edith: Oh, you know Mary. She likes to
be in at the kill.

Robert: She thinks if you put a toy down, it'll
still be sitting there when you want to play
with it again.

Edith: You think yourself so superior,
don't you?
Mary: Why not? I am.

Carson: She gave me a kiss in full payment.
Mrs Hughes: Then she had the better bargain.

Branson: He's a bit of a rough diamond.
Mary: I'm very fond of diamonds.

Branson: You know you're much nicer
than a lot of people realise.
Mary: Not always. Good night.

Robert: It's all right, Carson.
There's no point in even pretending
we can argue with Lady Mary.
Either of us.

Thomas: It's no use ganging up with Mr Molesley.
He can't protect you like I can. He doesn't know
what I know, does he?
Baxter: He knows how to be kind, Mr Barrow.
He has the advantage of you there.

ON ROBERT

Robert: No one has sharper eyes
than a loving son.

Robert: I'm a foolish man who's lost his way, and
I don't quite know how to find it again.

Violet: When you talk like that I'm tempted to
ring for Nanny and have you put to bed with
no supper.

Edith: Compared to Papa, you're a famous
chef . . . Really. He can't boil a kettle. If the
servants left he'd be found in a passage, dead,
arms stretched out, looking for the kitchen.

Mary: I'm impressed. My darling Papa
transformed into Machiavelli at a touch.
Will wonders never cease?

ON ROSAMUND

Violet: It's classic Rosamund. She's never more
righteous than when she's in the wrong.

Rosamund: I'm sorry, Mama, but you know me.
I have to say what I think.
Violet: Why? Nobody else does.

ON THOMAS

Baxter: You are your own worst enemy.
Thomas: If I am, I've got competition.

O'Brien: Watch yourself, Mr Bates.
Thomas is in charge now, and it won't do
to get on the wrong side of him.
Bates: Is there a right side?

Thomas: I'm just trying to be helpful.
Mrs Patmore: I'm afraid 'being helpful' is not
something we associate you with.

Edna: Do you ever wonder why people dislike
you so much? It's because you are sly and oily
and smug. And I'm really pleased I got the
chance to tell you before I go.
Thomas: Well, if we're playing the truth game, then you're a
manipulative little witch, and if your schemes have come to
nothing, I'm delighted.

Thomas: Don't do anything I wouldn't do.
Mrs Patmore: That gives you a bit of leeway.

Violet: Well, Lord Sinderby, Branson and Barrow. Not
what I call a recipe for a peaceful week's shooting.
Isobel: Makes you wonder what they'll be shooting
at by the end of it.

ON VIOLET

Robert: Mama is an old intriguer. She
will use tears or terror with equal facility.

Robert: Mama is not a good loser.
Cora: She's had so little experience.

Violet: So now I'm an outsider who
need not be consulted?
Cora: Since you put it like that, yes.

Cora: I think Granny's right.
Violet: Can somebody write that down?

Violet: I won't take sides, it's true, but I don't
think I could ever be described as 'neutral'.

Robert: You should be proud. Five years ago,
would you have believed you could be friendly
with my mother?
Branson: I'm not sure I'd have believed
it five minutes ago.

Carson: What 'old lady' are you referring to, Thomas? You cannot mean her ladyship the Dowager Countess. Not if you wish to remain in this house.